GRAHAM WARD

William Packwood, Tailor and Baptist Preacher

"... you will be my witnesses in Jerusalem and in all Judea and Samaria, and to the end of the earth." Acts 1:8

or, why did my 3 x Great-grandfather emigrate to New York?

Contents

Acknowledgement

My thanks to those who have contributed directly and indirectly to this work. In particular to the Wollaston Heritage Society and Marie Shelton of Wollaston Baptist Church.

This book is dedicated to the Wollaston families and their descendants who have been players in his unfolding story.

The cover illustration is from *Panorama of the Harbor of New York. Staten Island and the Narrows*, circa 1854. Image courtesy of New York Public Library.

Introduction

This short monograph traces the Christian calling of one William Packwood, a tailor turned Baptist preacher in the early 19th century in Northamptonshire, Bedfordshire and subsequently to America. It also explores the related context of nonconformity, especially that of Baptists in and around Wollaston before the formation of Wollaston Baptist Church.

William Packwood is a direct ancestor of the author and his descendants have continued in membership of Wollaston Baptist Church for close to 200 years.

Understanding the relationships within the Packwood family in Rushden and Wollaston is a challenge because of the repeated use of the same Christian names: John, William and Thomas through the generations and across different branches of the family. Many in the family also worked in tailoring adding to the difficulties of identifying specific individuals. Referring to the simplified family tree should provide some clarity.

WILLIAM PACKWOOD, TAILOR AND BAPTIST PREACHER

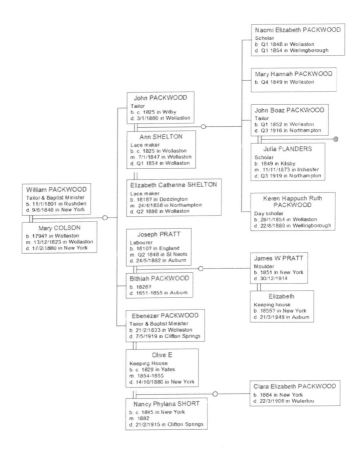

Naomi Elizabeth PACKWOOD
Scholar
b. Q1 1848 in Wollaston
d. Q1 1854 in Wellingborough

Mary Hannah PACKWOOD
b. Q4 1849 in Wollaston

John PACKWOOD
Tailor
b. c. 1825 in Wilby
d. 3/1/1880 in Wollaston

Ann SHELTON
Lace maker
b. c. 1825 in Wollaston
m. 7/1/1847 in Wollaston
d. Q1 1854 in Wollaston

John Boaz PACKWOOD
Tailor
b. Q1 1852 in Wollaston
d. Q3 1916 in Northampton

Julia FLANDERS
Scholar
b. 1849 in Kilsby
m. 11/11/1873 in Irchester
d. Q3 1919 in Northampton

Elizabeth Catherine SHELTON
Lace maker
b. 1818? in Doddington
m. 24/4/1858 in Northampton
d. Q2 1888 in Wollaston

Keren Happuch Ruth PACKWOOD
Day scholar
b. 28/1/1854 in Wollaston
d. 22/8/1880 in Wellingborough

William PACKWOOD
Tailor & Baptist Minister
b. 11/1/1801 in Rushden
d. 9/6/1848 in New York

Mary COLSON
b. 1794? in Wollaston
m. 13/12/1823 in Wollaston
d. 17/2/1880 in New York

Joseph PRATT
Labourer
b. 1810? in England
m. Q2 1848 in St Neots
d. 24/5/1882 in Auburn

James W PRATT
Moulder
b. 1851 in New York
d. 30/12/1914

Bithiah PACKWOOD
b. 1826?
d. 1851-1855 in Auburn

Elizabeth
Keeping house
b. 1855? in New York
d. 21/3/1948 in Auburn

Ebenezer PACKWOOD
Tailor & Baptist Minister
b. 21/2/1833 in Wollaston
d. 7/5/1919 in Clifton Springs

Olive E
Keeping House
b. c. 1829 in Yates
m. 1854-1855
d. 14/10/1880 in New York

Clara Elizabeth PACKWOOD
b. 1884 in New York
d. 22/3/1908 in Waterloo

Nancy Phylana SHORT
b. c. 1845 in New York
m. 1882
d. 21/2/1915 in Clifton Springs

2

The Packwood Family

William Packwood was born on 11 January 1801[1] the son of John Packwood and Elizabeth Hobbs, he was christened at the Parish Church of St Mary, Rushden on 21 September of the same year. His father was the parish clerk and Elizabeth was his second wife. When William was born he had one older sibling, John, from his father's first marriage to Susannah Clark. John was 21 when William arrived and was working as a tailor. Tailoring and drapery was a popular choice of occupation in the family and continued in several of the family's branches through the 19th and into the 20th century. All of John's sons turned to tailoring except Joseph who succeeded his father as Parish Clerk.

A house in Rushden went with the role of parish clerk together with an office at the Parish Church. John would have been a well-respected member of the community and part of the Church of England organisation locally. Whilst this was a lay role, the Parish Clerk in addition to his administrative duties was often required to assist the clergy in conducting services. The functions of the Parish Clerk would later be curtailed by an

---

[1] Rushden Parish Register, Northamptonshire Record Office; Northampton, England; Reference Number: 285P/212

Act of Parliament in 1844, transferring some responsibilities to the curate.

Despite growing up in a family closely connected with the Anglican parish, William appears in the historical record when he is admitted as a member of the Old Baptist Church, known as the "Top Meeting" in Rushden on 30th October 1820.[2] This would have been a significant decision for William and he appears to have been the only member of his family in his generation to have joined the Baptists. However, we can speculate that membership may have been of short duration as the word "excluded" appears against his name but without a subsequent date. Various words with very specific meanings were used in nonconformist church records at this time. Some examples are 'dismissed' i.e. transferred to another, usually similar, church in another location; 'withdrawn' usually implying non-attendance, or possibly attendance elsewhere; and 'excluded' when the individual has left on account of theological differences or for some misdemeanour contravening the church's accepted rules of behaviour. Later events in William's life may shed some light on the circumstances of his moving on.

However, it was at Rushden's "Top Meeting" where William met his future wife Mary Colson. The Colson family had been associated with the Baptist cause in Rushden from before 1749 when a new covenant was signed by members.

---

[2] Old Baptist Church "Top Meeting" Church Book, page 112

Nonconformity in Northamptonshire and beyond

Before we can understand the context of William's role in Wollaston where he next appears in the early 1820's we need to outline the background to the growth of the Baptist community in the village. The present-day Wollaston Baptist church traces its beginnings as a church from 1835. However, there is evidence of Baptists in the village as far back as 1722. That story though starts in neighbouring Rushden.

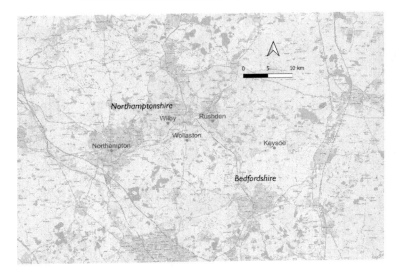

John Bunyan is remembered for his imprisonment for preaching and holding nonconformist conventicles[3] in the latter part of the 17th century when he wrote his famous Pilgrims Progress. He is also associated with an Independent[4] congregation in Bedford. What is less known is his extensive preaching in the villages in north Bedfordshire and Northamptonshire.

In March 1672, Charles II issued a Declaration of Indulgence which removed many of the restrictions on nonconformists. Protestant ministers that wanted to establish their own congregations, outside the Church of England, could do so if they applied for licences. It placed dissenting ministers and their communities in an acute dilemma: if they applied for a licence to set up a dissenting conventicle, they would be implicitly acknowledging a royal authority that many regarded as illegal,

---

3 An unlawful religious meeting, typically of nonconformists

4 Independents later became known as Congregationalists

as well as associating themselves with Catholic liberty and the attack on one of Europe's foremost Protestant powers. Nevertheless, thousands did and enjoyed for a brief time a flourishing culture of free nonconformist worship.

This system devised by the state to control such activity, making it necessary to apply for a licence to meet in each specific locality is now a primary source for tracing these early nonconformist congregations. A licence for Wollaston bears the initials 'J.B.' and is presumed to be in John Bunyan's hand, so we can be reasonably certain that he preached in John Morice's barn in 1672.[5]

Rushden

Meetings in Rushden and Wollaston continued into the 1680s with more relaxed legal restrictions put upon them. These seem to have come about from the efforts of the Baptist meeting at Stevington, another Bunyan-inspired congregation, which was particularly successful in having members across a wide area even as far away as Northampton. In time, these satellite groups established themselves as independent congregations. By 1686 regular meetings were taking place in Rushden and Wollaston but remained under the oversight of Stevington by their pastors Stephen Hawthorne and Daniel Negus. In 1689 nonconformist congregations were finally able to meet freely under the conditions of the Toleration Act and were no longer required to pay fines for non-attendance at the parish church.

Probably in 1722, a Baptist church was constituted at Rushden together with a branch congregation meeting at Wollaston. This

---

[5] Calendar of State Papers Domestic, 1672

was likely an open communion and open membership church, accepting as members both baptised adult believers and others on expression of faith. The earliest entries in the church book are the church accounts for 1723 in the handwriting of the pastor, John Wollaston, who is later described as 'minister of the Church of Christ meeting at Rushden and Wollaston of the Strict Baptist Denomination'. A significant change occurred in 1735 when a new covenant between members was agreed upon, forgoing the open communion and open membership principles for a strict communion position:

'We do solemnly declare that we do love & esteem all them that love and serve the Lord Jesus Christ in sincerity, & although they differ from us in some things, we can hold conference with them, Joyne in prayers, heare such preach that are sound in ye doctrines of ye gospel. But cannot sit down in full communion though we believe them to be & have the essence of a gospel Church, but not Regular Sitting down at the Lord's Table with unbaptized persons which practise we Judge unwarrantable for many good and substantial Reasons.'

Issues of qualification for church membership, whether communion was open to all or only baptised members of a specific congregation and the extent to which the theology expressed by the pastor and congregation was 'Calvinistic' or not frequently swung to and fro, particularly on the appointment of a new pastor. This often led to splits in congregations and the planting of new churches in the same locality.

John Wollaston died in 1737 and the new church state did not last long as a new covenant was agreed in 1749 reverting in part to the original foundation document of the church. However, the minutes show that at this time members were not 'all of a mind with respect to the ordinance of Baptism' but agreed all 'their Liberty to act according to their conscience therein without offence'. The church had declined since its formation 27 years previously as only eleven of the original members signed. The issue of membership and communion continued to be one that was to recur over the years with this and associated congregations into the 19th century.

From 1749 William Knowles of Keysoe preached frequently at the Rushden meeting and in 1752 was ordained pastor. William had a successful time at Rushden and was in demand as a visiting preacher elsewhere as his diary (1767-1787) confirms. He also frequently preached at Wollaston.

The subject of the covenant between members was again re-considered in 1768 but the general position on baptism remained unchanged:

not to 'lord it over the consciences of our brethren, knowing that whatsoever is not faith is sin'.

An accommodation

It is perhaps surprising that a group of Baptists could agree to meet together when holding different positions on such fundamental issues. This was however not unique in Baptist churches at the time. College Lane (later College Street) Baptist church in Northampton had adopted a similar position at a church meeting on November 18th, 1700, the record states:

Whereas this Church professeth Mixt Communion (as to matter of Judgement about Water Baptism). It was agreed upon & passed as an Act (Nem: Contrad:) That a few Lines should be inserted in the Church Book, & annexed to the Covenant, wherein our Members unanimously do solemnly Testify & Engage not to Impose or Reflect on one another, as touching that matter, &c.

The lines annexed to the Church Covenant were:

And whereas we differ in our Judgments about Water-Baptism, We do now Solemnly declare, That we that are for Infant Baptism do not hereby, nor will not impose on the others or any of our Brethren or Sisters that are among us who, are for Baptism upon Profession of Faith. And on the other hand, We that are for Believers Baptism do not, nor will not impose upon the Consciences of any of our Brethren or Sisters that are amongst us, that are for Infant Baptism. Nor will we (either Party, or any of us) impose upon any that hereafter may joyn in Communion with us; But do all promise (freely & cordially, without casting Reflections, &c., on the Persons or Practice of any) to leave everyone to his or her Liberty of Judgment & Practice herein; Each of us walking Conscientiously up to our Light; Engaging & Endeavouring in the Strength of Christ that our difference in Judgement shall not cause Breach of Union or Affection.

On Calvinism

Apart from differing views on baptism and communion, Baptists also held differing views on Calvinism. The Rushden church was not part of the Northamptonshire Baptist Association to which the majority of local churches belonged which had been formed in 1764. There were several churches in the county among them Rushden, Irthlingborough, Raunds and Northampton's second Baptist church (Fish Street, later Abington Street) who all held to a Calvinist theology. Rushden did eventually join the Association, but not until 1844. Towards the end of the 18th and early 19th centuries, the Association was led by figures like Andrew Fuller of Kettering, John Ryland of Northampton and

John Sutcliff of Olney. An interesting exchange between the Rushden and Kettering churches arose as the consequence of an application for the transfer of a member, Mrs Wright, from Rushden to Kettering.

The Rushden church in the summer of 1785 refused to provide a letter of dismission to Mrs. Wright to join the Kettering church. Andrew Fuller had commented in his diary earlier in February 1785 in respect of relations between the two churches:

'the people at Rushden carry their resentments very high on account of what they reckon my erroneous principles. I need grace not so much at present to keep me from resenting again as to keep me from rejoicing in their iniquity. Undoubtedly they could not take measures that would more conduce to the reputation of what I have written, and of what I preach, as well as against themselves.'

Later, on 16th July 1785, he wrote:

"the system of religion which he [William Knowles, pastor of Rushden] and many others embibe enervates every species of vital godliness!"

A letter from the Rushden church to the Kettering church in September 1785 complained that the Kettering congregation

"having gone off from their former principles."

This was interpreted by Andrew Fuller to mean that he and the church had departed from "Calvinistical principles". The Kettering church replied with a letter to the Rushden church that they were:

"not conscious of having departed, or of being in the least inclined to depart from any one of them."

Rushden eventually conceded the point but not until 1796 when Mrs. Wright was finally given her letter of dismission from Rushden to Kettering.

Wollaston

The first Wollaston Baptist church met on London Road near the former 'Marquis of Granby' public house[6] around 1735. The Rushden and Wollaston meetings shared a pastor who came to Wollaston every 2 or 3 weeks. Because of poor attendance, Ambrose Dickins, the lord of the manor, closed the church in 1750 and converted it to a bath-house. It was still referred to as a 'cold bath' at the time of enclosure in 1789. After closure, the enthusiasm of Rebecca Rose, and John Luddington urged the remaining Baptists to attend the Rushden meeting despite the difficulties of travelling.

Soon after, in 1752 an Independent Church was also formed in Wollaston. This church would have been open communion and would not have been exercised by the baptism question. It grew into a thriving meeting, it too with congregations meeting in other villages in the area. In 1835 the Independents recorded 9 baptisms, including one adult; interesting for this story as it was a member of the Colson family, Sophia Colson daughter of Benjamin and Hannah Colson. A Sophia Colson was a witness to both the marriage of William Packwood and Mary Colson in December 1823 and also of William Colson and Mary Lucy in Wollaston in June of the same year. It would not be unreasonable to assume that William, Mary and Sophia were all children of Benjamin and Hannah Colson. The Independent meeting continued until 1923. Its meeting place still stands and is now the home of the Wollaston Museum.

During the second half of the 18th century mention of Baptists

---

6 The site is now a private house "The Old Marquis" on London Road, Wollaston.

in Wollaston Baptists in the historical record is scant, but they may have continued to meet for some time. Still, in 1822 a few like-minded individuals, Joseph Knighton, William Packwood, Benjamin Brown, and John Luddington, 'Were led to assemble together for prayer at our friend Brown's dwelling place.' in the High Street opposite the Post Office. A formal Baptist church was not re-established in Wollaston until 1834.

William Packwood in Wollaston and beyond

Wollaston and Wilby

William married Mary Colson in 1823 at Wollaston Parish Church[7], but William gave his address as Wilby just four miles from Wollaston. Their first son John was also born in Wilby in about 1825 but their next child, a daughter, Bithiah was born back at Wollaston in about 1826 as was their second son, Ebenezer in 1833. None of their children were christened at local parish churches which is perhaps not surprising given their parents' connections with the Baptist cause at Wollaston. Noting the gaps in the ages of the children we could speculate that other children may have been born between 1826 and 1833 but did not survive infancy. These three children appear together as a family in the 1841 census.

An unanswered question is why was William living in Wilby when he had a connection with the Baptist meeting he was leading in Wollaston. In 1823 he would have been aged 22 and would probably have completed his apprenticeship as a tailor

---

[7] In 1822 nonconformists were still required to marry in the parish church

the previous year. At this time he may have still been working for his previous master, however, by 1826 they had returned to Wollaston. There do not appear to be any relevant surviving apprenticeship records for the period in this area that might clarify his movements.

William and Mary probably remained in Wollaston until 1832 as William is listed in the poll for the parliamentary election in December 1832.

Early Wollaston meetings

William Packwood spoke at this small meeting for 7 or 8 years but without any significant success. The friends at that time did not experience significant growth in attendance. Sometimes those who did attend were few, perhaps 12 to 20 in the congregation and at other times just two praying men and three others.[8]

Meetings were discontinued for a couple of years, but faithful friends started to meet again and soon three of four young people joined the gathering. This was probably in 1833.

They were greatly encouraged by John Robinson of Turvey, giving £40 to build a chapel. John Robinson, a lacemaker, had been similarly generous in providing £150 for a manse for Stevington Baptist Church in 1832. Mrs Andrews gave £50 to purchase additional land and John Robinson gave a further £15 for the vestry and baptistry. Some time previously Joseph Knighton and William Packwood had each contributed £2 10 shillings to obtain the plot known as the "old coach road", this was subsequently exchanged by Samuel Robinson of Wilby for the piece of ground the original chapel stood on.

---

[8] Wollaston Baptist Church Centenary booklet (1834)

Mr Meakins, of Northampton, was 'the first regular pastor of the new chapel, and served for nine years. A long solemn covenant was drawn up laying down the duties of Church members:

"And having, as we hope first given our own selves to the Lord, we judge it our duty to be giving ourselves to each other by the will of God, to walk together in a visible Church state, laying the foundation upon the person, office, authority, spirit, and word of Christ - especially these two great institutions, Baptism and the Supper of' the Lord."

The names of those who attended Communion on June 21st, 1835, were: Sarah Waples, Elizabeth Saunders, Benjamin Brown, John Saunders, William Berrill, James Tye, John Luddingtcn, and Joseph Knighton. Several of whom had prayed together for this day over the previous 13 years.

The appointment of Mr Meakins as the first pastor indicates as to the theological position of the new church. Meakins had only been appointed to the position of a new meeting in Chapel Place, St Edmund's End, Northampton on 7 October 1834. This was a new cause that appears to have broken away from the Strict Baptist church in Abington Street, Northampton. Among the the local pastors taking part in the ordination service were John Whittemore of Succoth Chapel, Rushden, James Trimming of Irthlingborough and John Woolston of Keysoe Row who had himself only two weeks previously (30th September) been ordained at Keysoe having been sent from Succoth chapel at Rushden. All of these men were well-known Strict Baptist pastors.[9]

---

[9]   Gospel Herald, 1834, 261-262

The 1834 chapel is shown here on the right. A new chapel was built in 1868 to the west and set back from the original building in 1867. This was further extended in 1933. Both buildings were demolished and replaced by a new building in 2012.

Map (1884) showing the location of the first known Baptist meeting and later chapel buildings (1834 and 1867)

Keysoe, Bedfordshire

The Packwood family's next appearance in the historical record is in Keysoe across the border in Bedfordshire in 1833. William is recorded as paying the parish poor rate. Keysoe is 13 miles from Wollaston and not the most obvious destination from Wollaston. Keysoe had a population of 701 which had almost doubled since 1801. The choice of Keysoe probably lies in the fact that although it was a small village it was the location of two existing Baptist churches, Keysoe Brook End and Keysoe Row. Brook End was much the oldest tracing its beginnings before the days of John Bunyan in 1652. The chapel at Brook End practised "mixed communion", that is, members were admitted either after adult baptism or after a profession of faith. In 1808 a group led by Joel Miles who had left Brook End in 1801 started a meeting in a barn owned by him and formally established themselves as a Baptist Church in 1812. Here all new members were baptised by full immersion in a pool behind the chapel.

Soon after they arrived in Keysoe their second son, Ebenezer arrived in February 1833.

It could be assumed that the Packwoods attended one of these two meetings however they may not have been to their liking as on 21st December 1838 the house of Mr Samuel Whitmee in Keysoe Row was registered by Whitmee himself, Eli Shelford and William Packwood as a meeting house.[10] Was there room for another Baptist meeting in Keysoe? Probably, if we consider William's departure from Rushden's "Top Meeting" ten years or so previously. It is likely that William Packwood held firm Calvinistic views and practised closed communion, i.e. com-

---

[10] Bedfordshire & Luton archives, ABN1/2; ABN2/334

munion was restricted to believers who had been baptised by full immersion and accepted into membership of their local congregation.

There now follows a frustrating gap in the historical record and we can only assume that the Packwood family remained in Keysoe for the next few years. The 1841 census shows William, Mary, Bithiah and Ebenezer living in Keysoe and William working as a tailor. The census also suggests that Ebenezer was not born in Bedfordshire, implying he was born whilst they were still in Wollaston. It would not be unusual for someone to pastor a small congregation and continue in a trade at the same time, as evidenced by many like the cobbler-missionary, William Carey at Moulton. In 1841 William and Mary's son John Packwood, although only 15 was living with a cousin and his parents back in Wollaston. This was another tailor family and John was likely at this time learning his future trade.

John married Ann Shelton in 1847 a family long associated with the Baptists in Wollaston and whose mother was from the Knighton family. Her brother Joseph had been instrumental in the founding of the Wollaston Baptist cause. Sadly Ann died in 1854, probably during the birth of her fourth child, Keren Happuch Ruth Packwood in January 1854. In 1858 John Pack-wood remarried, this time to Ann's older step-sister Elizabeth Catherine Shelton.

John was to continue his trade in Wollaston until 1880 when he died in tragic circumstances as a suicide. He had had a history of mental illness having spent 15 months in the Northampton Asylum about 1859.[11]

---

[11] Northampton Mercury. 10 January 1880

To New York

William was, as has been indicated, part of an extended family of Packwood from Rushden, Wollaston and Melchbourne in Bedfordshire. It was another William Packwood a cousin and 15 years older than William, the tailor of Rushden who we now need to follow for a few years.

This William of Melchbourne, a farmer, emigrated to New York in 1830 with his wife and six children aged between 6 months and 13 years. In the spring 1830 they sailed from Liverpool on a ship the 'Courier' and arrived in New York in May 1830 and settled in Auburn, Cayuga County, New York. Cayuga County borders the southern shore of Lake Ontario.

It was almost certainly this cousin's experience that prompted William then living in Keysoe to also emigrate with his family to New York. The 19th- century was a time of significant migration to the States that only increased as the decades passed. For William in Keysoe, it offered the opportunity of a new life in a growing country which was sure to offer good prospects for him both as a tailor and a Christian leader. His family too departed from Liverpool aboard the 'Courier' on 25 April 1848 for St John, New Brunswick and Staten Island (New York). The party comprised of William and his wife Mary, daughter Bithiah and her husband Joseph Pratt who had only been married a few weeks earlier, together with 15-year-old Ebenezer Packwood. William, Ebenezer and Joseph Pratt were all described as labourers, although this may not be significant as the two wives were described as 'spinsters'.

The 'Courier', by artist James Guy Evans (c.1810–1859)

Identifying the actual ship that crossed from Liverpool to Staten Island is more of a challenge than it would first appear as at any one time there could be several ships by the same name following similar routes. The fact that both these families travelled on a ship called 'Courier' eighteen years apart does not confirm this one way or another. The 1830 voyage was undertaken by a small ship of 388 tons that had commenced its Atlantic crossing schedule in 1824. Another ship called the 'Courier' at 1060 tons was built at St John, New Brunswick in 1847 and was also deployed on Atlantic crossings from Liverpool.

The ship's passenger list recorded the Courier being docked

at Staten Island on 14th June 1848[12] having travelled via St John, New Brunswick. However, press reports and Lloyd's List reports indicate that the ship arrived on 9th June.[13] These dates are significant as tragedy struck on the day of arrival or shortly afterwards.

---

[12] Passenger List: Arrival: New York, New York, Year: 1848, (Year: 1848; Arrival: New York, New York; Microfilm Serial: M237, 1820-1897; Microfilm Roll: Roll 073; Line: 33; List Number: 566; Page Number: 8). Ancestry.com.

[13] Shipping and Mercantile Gazette, Saturday 24 June 1848
  Lloyd's List, Monday 26 June 1848

A gravestone in North Street Cemetery, Auburn records the death of William Packwood. Close inspection reveals some interesting facts. The date of death is given as 9 June 1848. If this is accurate this is the date the 'Courier' arrived at Staten Island. The ship's passenger list does not indicate that he had died on board so it probably occurred soon after. The second point is that the gravestone describes him as "Rev" William Packwood. This is unusual in two respects. It does not quite fit with his presumed Calvinistic theology it would be more common for a church leader of such a group to shun such titles. There is also no evidence that William was ordained at any of the causes he pastored.

It is not surprising to find that after William's death his widow, Mary and her two children settled in Auburn where William's cousin had settled 18 years previously and was still living.

The legacy

This story does not end here!

William's story does not end in total tragedy. In the 1850 US census, we find the remaining family living in Auburn, only a short distance away from William's older cousin and family. The family comprised of Joseph and Bithiah Pratt, Mary Packwood and her son Ebenezer Packwood. Ebenezer, now 17, was described as a tailor.

By the time of the next census in 1855 Bithiah had died and the family was reduced to Joseph Pratt, his son James aged 4, and his mother-in-law Mary Packwood. Ebenezer had now married a lady by the name of Olive and had only moved a short distance from his mother and the Pratt family within the same district (Ward 2) in Auburn. He was still working as a tailor.

In 1860 we find Ebenezer had given up his tailoring business and was living in Rochester, Monroe County, New York with his wife Olive. Ebenezer was now a Divinity Student at the Rochester Theological Seminary (RTS). RTS had been founded in 1850 alongside the University of Rochester as a college for primarily Baptist ministerial students.

Postcard of Rochester Theological Seminary in 1911

He probably commenced his studies in 1858-59 and graduated in 1861. This year marked the start of the American Civil War (12 April 1861 – 26 May 1865). Ebenezer enlisted in the Union army in York, Livingston County, New York in July 1863. At this point, he was described as a minister, but it is not known whether this assigned him to non-combative duties.

In the 1865 census, he was described as a Baptist clergyman in York with his wife and mother. Over the following years, he served as pastor in several Baptist churches across New York and Pennsylvania.[14]

---

[14] Biography, University of Rochester, 1850-1928, Ebenezer Packwood
https://rbscp.lib.rochester.edu/alumni-records/browse

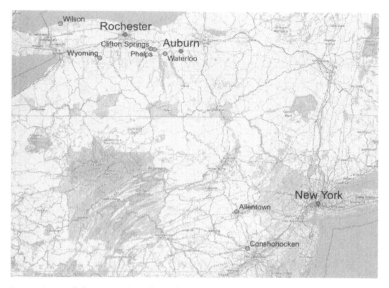

Location of the Baptist churches where Ebenezer Packwood was pastor

Sadly in 1880 Ebenezer's wife, Olive died. In 1882 he married Nancy Short a member of his congregation. Then followed the arrival of a daughter Clara Elizabeth Packwood. By 1895 he appears to have retired from full-time pastorate at Waterloo as he then describes himself as a farmer although he does still describe himself as a minister from time to time. In 1908 his daughter Clara died and later that year in July, the couple sold their property and moved back to Clifton Springs. His wife Nancy died in 1915 and Ebenezer continued to live at Clifton Springs until he died in 1919.

There are no living descendants of this American line of the family.

Wollaston Baptist Church in Northamptonshire continues to serve its community into the 21st century.

Printed in Great Britain
by Amazon

32580451R00020